AMERICA'S BLOODY BEGINNINGS

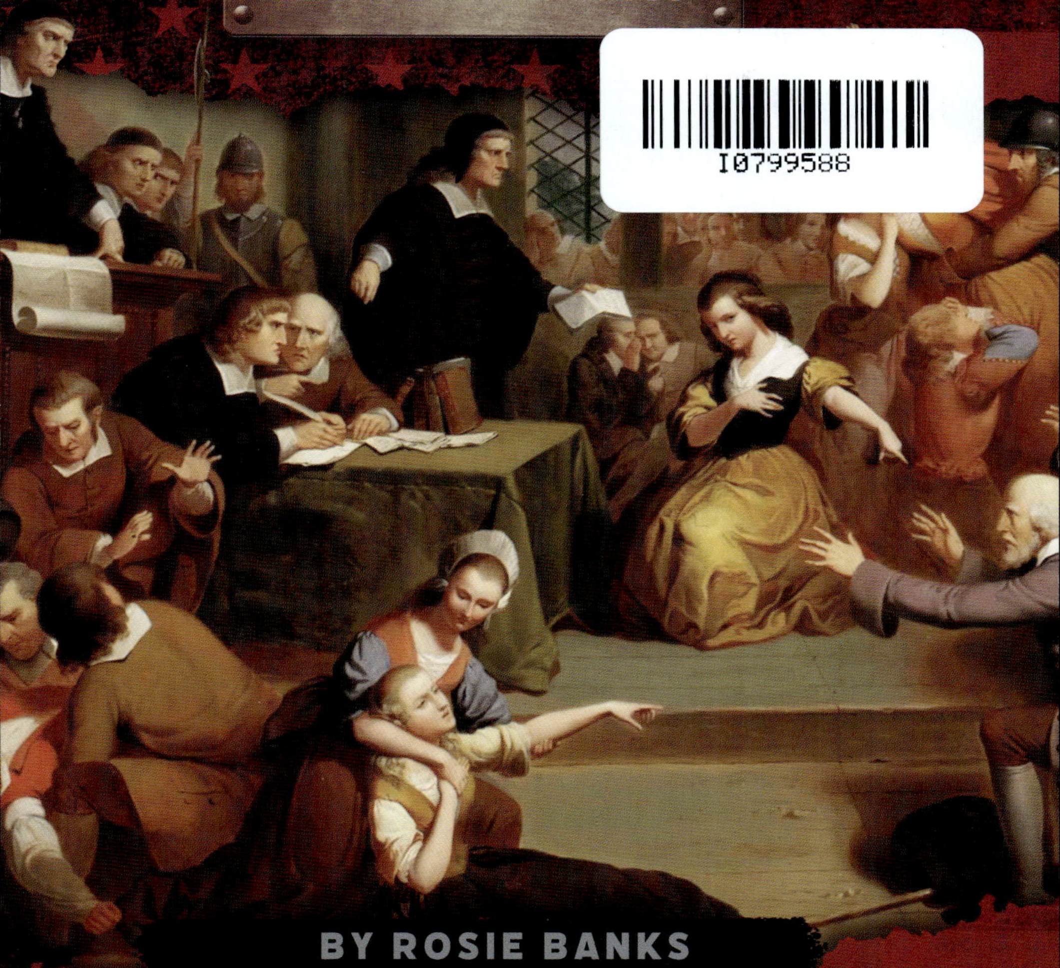

BY ROSIE BANKS

THE SALEM WITCH TRIALS

Gareth Stevens
PUBLISHING

Please visit our website, www.garethstevens.com. For a free color catalog of all our high-quality books, call toll free 1-800-542-2595 or fax 1-877-542-2596.

Library of Congress Cataloging-in-Publication Data
Names: Banks, Rosie, 1978- author.
Title: The Salem witch trials / Rosie Banks.
Description: Buffalo : Gareth Stevens Publishing, 2026. | Series: America's bloody beginnings | Includes index.
Identifiers: LCCN 2025000216 (print) | LCCN 2025000217 (ebook) | ISBN 9781482472356 (library binding) | ISBN 9781482472349 (paperback) | ISBN 9781482472363 (ebook)
Subjects: LCSH: Trials (Witchcraft)–Massachusetts–Salem–Juvenile literature. | Trials (Witchcraft)–Massachusetts–Salem–History–17th century–Juvenile literature. | Witchcraft–Massachusetts–Salem–History–Juvenile literature. | Salem (Mass.)–History–Colonial period, ca. 1600-1775–Juvenile literature. | Salem (Mass.)–Social conditions–Juvenile literature.
Classification: LCC KFM2478.8.W5 B355 2026 (print) | LCC KFM2478.8.W5 (ebook) | DDC 345.744/50288–dc23/eng/20250107
LC record available at https://lccn.loc.gov/2025000216
LC ebook record available at https://lccn.loc.gov/2025000217

Published in 2026 by
Gareth Stevens Publishing
2544 Clinton Street
Buffalo, NY 14224

Designer: Leslie Taylor
Editor: Therese Shea

Photo credits: Cover (photo) Thomkins H. Matteson/File:Matteson-jacobs.jpg_commons.wikimedia.org; (series art red texture) Sittipol sukuna/Shutterstock.com; (series art flag) Fedorov Oleksiy/Shutterstock.com; (series art ripped paper) Paul C. Ware/Shutterstock.com; (series art metal plate) Allgusak/Shutterstock.com; (series art caption flag) Rikley Stock/Shutterstock.com; p. 5 W.P. Upham/File:Salem Village - map of - Project Gutenberg eText 17845.jpg_commons.wikimedia.org; p. 7 Wellcome Images/ File:Witches apprehended...,1613 Wellcome M0016701.jpg_commons.wikimedia.org; p. 9 (Samuel Parris) Massachusetts Historical Society/File:Samuel Parris.jpeg_commons.wikimedia.org, (Tituba) Henry Wadsworth Longfellow/File:Tituba-Longfellow-Corey_commons.wikimedia.org; p. 11 (top) Everett Collection/Shutterstock.com, (bottom) Henrietta D. Kimball/File:HouseWhereWitchcraftStarted.png_commons.wikimedia.org; p. 13 Unknown Author/File:Jonathan Corwin Portrait.jpg_commons.wikimedia.org; p. 15 Harvard University Museums of Art/File:WilliamStoughton.jpg_commons.wikimedia.org; (inset) Freeland A. Carter/File:RebeccaNurse-inChains.jpg_commons.wikimedia.org; p. 17 Howard Pyle/File:There is a flock of yellow birds around her head.jpg_commons.wikimedia.org; p. 19 (top) Willjay/File:RebeccaNurseHouse2006.jpg_commons.wikimedia.org, (Bridget Bishop) Unknown Author/File:Bridget Bishop.jpg_commons.wikimedia.org, (execution) Internet Archive Book Images/Flickr.com; p. 21 (top) Ridpath/File:Giles Corey restored.jpg_commons.wikimedia.org, (bottom) Remisser/File:Gilescoreymemorial.jpg_commons.wikimedia.org; p. 23 T. H. Matteson/File:Examination of a Witch - Tompkins Matteson.jpg_commons.wikimedia.org; p. 25 (top) Matthias Jiury Rabbione/Shutterstock.com, (Cotton Mather) Everett Collection/Shutterstock.com, (publication) Cotton Mather/File:WondersoftheInvisibleWorld-1693.jpg_commons.wikimedia.org; p. 27 Francis Helminski/File:Danvers victims memorial, quotations from victims.jpg_commons.wikimedia.org; p. 29 Sarah Jennie/Shutterstock.com.

Printed in the United States of America

CPSIA compliance information: Batch #CS26GS: For further information, contact Gareth Stevens Publishing at 1-800-542-2595.

CONTENTS

A Colonial Crisis 4
Witch Hunts 6
Setting the Scene in Salem 8
Many More Accused 14
On Trial 16
Death Sentences 18
An End to the Trials 22
If Not Witchcraft, What? 24
Aftermath 26
The Last Witch 28
Glossary 30
For More Information 31
Index 32

Words in the glossary appear in **bold** the first time they are used in the text.

A COLONIAL CRISIS

Few incidents in colonial history have captured modern imaginations like the Salem witch trials of the late 1600s have. People wonder what really happened in Salem Village in the colony of Massachusetts to cause 19 people to be **convicted** of witchcraft—and hanged for it.

To understand how these events occurred, it's important to know what was happening in the North American colonies and around the world at that time. Belief in witchcraft had been widespread. And when bad things occurred, people often looked for **supernatural** reasons rather than scientific reasons. Sometimes, this resulted in witch hunts, which placed blame on innocent people.

Salem Village was renamed Danvers in 1752. The town of Salem, which is still called Salem, is in the lower-right corner of this map, marked with a star.

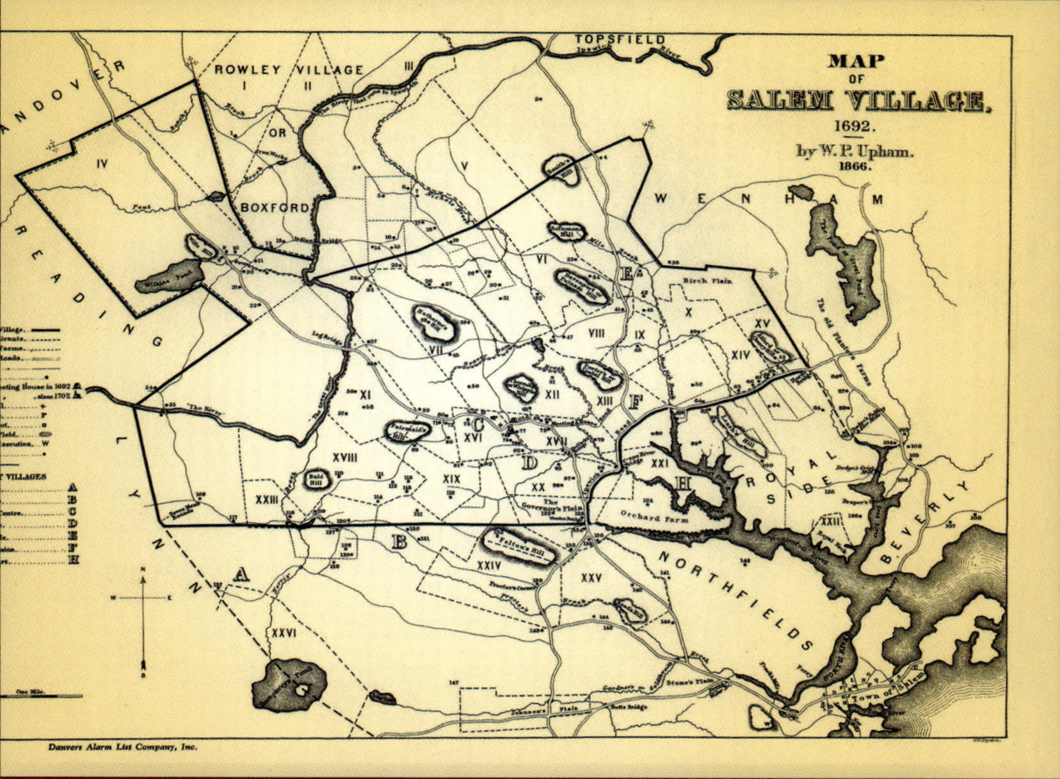

WHAT'S A WITCH?

Witches were thought to be people who had evil powers because they were followers of evil spirits or beings. It was believed that witches could change from human to animal form. Both men and women could be accused of witchcraft—though women were accused much more.

WITCH HUNTS

Witch hunts weren't unique, or special, to the North American colonies. Witch hunts were recorded in Europe as early as the 1300s and were an ongoing occurrence throughout the centuries that followed. Most witch hunts on that continent took place in today's Germany, France, Netherlands, Belgium, Luxembourg, Italy, and Switzerland. Historians still argue about how many people were accused, but some say about 110,000 were put on trial and perhaps as many as 60,000 were found guilty and executed, or killed.

By the time of the tragic events of Salem Village in the 17th century, witch hunts in Europe were coming to an end. However, European settlers had brought beliefs in witchcraft with them to the colonies.

Witches Apprehended, Examined and Executed, for notable villanies by them committed both by Land and Water.

With a ſtrange and moſt true triall how to know whether a woman be a Witch or not.

This **pamphlet** tells of women being accused and found guilty of witchcraft in England in 1613. In 1736, Britain passed an act ending laws against witchcraft, which had been used to put over 500 people to death over the years.

WHAT WERE WITCHES ACCUSED OF?

Witch hunts in **medieval** Europe took place during times of trouble, such as wars and epidemics, or widespread diseases. Witches were accused of causing deaths, sicknesses, pains, bad weather, failed crops, and many other misfortunes. These were times in which knowledge of science was limited.

SETTING THE SCENE IN SALEM

In the late 1600s, Salem Village was a farming community. It was less wealthy than the nearby port of Salem Town (today's Salem, Massachusetts). It had about 500 villagers. The most **prominent** were from two families: the Porters and the Putnams. The community was known as a place where people argued and took others to court over many matters.

In 1689, the Putnams supported Samuel Parris becoming the pastor, or religious leader, of Salem Village's Congregational church. Parris had lived in Barbados, a country in the Caribbean. He moved to Salem Village with his family and two enslaved people from Barbados: a man named John Indian and a woman named Tituba.

No one is sure what Tituba looked like or even where she came from. Some think she was Native American because of her name. Others think she was African. She played a large role in the witch trials.

Samuel Parris

Tituba

PARRIS THE PURITAN

Samuel Parris was a Puritan. Puritans were people who wanted to simplify the Church of England. Some had left Europe in order to practice their religious beliefs without persecution, or punishment. The Pilgrims were a mostly Puritan group that left England and established the Massachusetts Bay Colony in the 1630s.

Parris's leadership of Salem Village's church only increased the arguments in the community. Parris wanted more payment and ownership of the pastor's house, for example. And he made people who weren't members of the church leave during a certain part of the service. Salem Village soon was divided along the lines of those who supported Parris and those who didn't.

In 1692, Betty Parris, the nine-year-old daughter of Samuel, and Abigail Williams, his eleven-year-old niece, began to display odd behaviors. These included periods of screaming, twisting into odd shapes, and throwing things. They also reported feeling something—or someone—pinch and bite them.

In this illustration of a witch trial, a young woman convulses, or shakes, on the floor while another woman defends herself from witchcraft in court.

house of Pastor Samuel Parris

THE DOCTOR'S VISIT

Betty Parris and Abigail Williams were examined by the local doctor, William Griggs, who could find no reason for their behavior. Some think Griggs had little training as a doctor. It may have been Griggs who suggested supernatural reasons for what was happening to them.

Now suspecting witchcraft, Samuel Parris asked the girls who was causing their behaviors. They blamed three women: the enslaved woman Tituba, a poor woman named Sarah Good, and an elderly woman named Sarah Osborn.

Two **magistrates** arrived from Salem Town on March 1. Good and Osborn denied the charges against them, but Good accused Osborn of witchcraft. Tituba also said she was innocent at first, but later said she was guilty. She may have been forced into the confession. She said she had talked with the Devil and saw a book of witches in which she saw the names of Good, Osborn, and seven others—though she couldn't read their names.

Jonathan Corwin, shown here, was one of the magistrates who came to hear the evidence, or proof, against Good, Osborn, and Tituba.

ON THE OUTSKIRTS

All three of the accused women had something in common—they were outsiders in the community. They didn't attend church, weren't liked by their neighbors, or were seen as different and therefore suspicious. **Marginalized** women like these were often viewed with distrust and even accused of witchcraft.

MANY MORE ACCUSED

Tituba's incomplete list of witches sparked fear in the community. Many claimed to have symptoms like the young girls had displayed. These new "victims" accused more people in the community of witchcraft, some of whom were prominent citizens, such as Rebecca Nurse. Samuel Parris also preached about witchcraft in church.

Historians have noted that of the more than 150 men and women who were accused and imprisoned in and near Salem, many were known to be enemies of the Putnam family. About three-fourths were women.

In May 1692, the governor of Massachusetts ordered that a special court be set up in Salem Town to oversee trials for the accused.

The special court was overseen by William Stoughton, who was also the colony's lieutenant governor.

Rebecca Nurse in chains

THE COURT OF OYER AND TERMINER

The court set up for the Salem witch trials was called the Court of Oyer and Terminer. This court could both hear the **testimony** and evidence and determine, or decide, whether the accused was innocent or guilty. The court had to have at least five judges present, most of whom were wealthy businessmen rather than men who had studied law.

supernatural or invisible.

If the accused admitted guilt, the court sometimes let them go, especially if they named others as witches. Those who were accused and maintained they were innocent faced death if found guilty.

Those who were on trial for witchcraft in Salem didn't have lawyers—they had to defend themselves.

MORE ABOUT SPECTRAL EVIDENCE

Spectral evidence was testimony that people gave about crimes being committed by spirits. Some claimed that people's spirits hurt them, made them sick, or did other things. This was nearly impossible to disprove as it didn't matter if the accused was miles away—their spirit was still believed to be capable of crimes.

DEATH SENTENCES

Bridget Bishop was the first person to be convicted, or found guilty, of witchcraft at the Salem trials. She denied wrongdoing, saying, "I am as innocent as an unborn child." She was hanged on June 10, 1692.

The next month, on July 19, five more people were hanged, including Sarah Good, one of the first accused. Rebecca Nurse, a well-respected church member, was another woman who was hanged that day. Many people came to court to defend her. The court even decided she was not guilty at first. However, her accusers—including members of the Putnam family—continued to say she was a witch. She was finally sentenced to death.

This was Rebecca Nurse's home, which still stands in today's Danvers, Massachusetts. It's said that her body was taken from a shallow grave and reburied near her home.

Bridget Bishop

execution of George Burroughs

CASTING DOUBT ON THE CONVICTION

On August 19, five more people were hanged. George Burroughs was one of these. He had been a minister in Salem. It was recorded that he said a prayer before he was hanged. Some thought this was proof that he was not a witch, as a witch could not say such a prayer. He was still killed that day, though.

On September 22, 1692, eight more people were hanged for witchcraft. A woman named Martha Corey was one of these. Martha's husband, Giles, was also accused. But he refused to enter a plea, which means to state whether he was guilty or innocent. This may have been a way to avoid the trial. However, it was permitted to try to force someone to enter a plea using an extreme method called *peine forte et dure* (French for "strong and hard punishment").

According to this process, Giles Corey had his clothing removed. He was forced to lay down. Wood boards were placed on his body. Then rocks were placed on the boards. More weight was added until he was crushed to death.

Giles Corey refused to enter a plea even after being pressed by heavy rocks. He finally died on September 19, 1692, at the age of 81.

STAYING SILENT

Not everyone in the Salem community believed in witchcraft. However, many were scared into silence. They worried if they called the accusers liars, they, too, would be accused and face the same dangers in a court in which people were assumed to be guilty, not innocent.

AN END TO THE TRIALS

It wasn't only people in Salem Village and Salem Town that were drawn into the trials. People in neighboring communities were also accused, including in Boston. One of the last people to be accused was the wife of Massachusetts Governor William Phips.

The governor soon ended the special court and began a new one that did not accept spectral evidence. This court heard trials for 56 more people at the beginning of 1693. Just three of these people were convicted. The trials finally came to an end. All the convicted who hadn't been executed were pardoned by the governor by May 1693.

Certain moles or other marks on someone's body were used as proof that someone was a witch.

OTHER KINDS OF EVIDENCE

Without spectral evidence, what other kinds of evidence did people offer of witchcraft? If someone confessed to be a witch and named someone else, that was considered evidence. Having a doll or figure thought to look like someone was also evidence. Having books about fortune-telling was also proof, in addition to mixtures, including natural healing lotions and medicines.

IF NOT WITCHCRAFT, WHAT?

While it's possible that some accusations of witchcraft were revenge, mistakes, or just fear, scientists have some other ideas. The odd behaviors and sudden pains of some of the villagers could have been due to certain diseases or conditions. It's also known that foods made of the grain called rye can be affected by the **fungus** ergot. When eaten by people, ergot can make them choke, throw up, and even **hallucinate**. So, some villagers may have really been experiencing something.

In addition, the minister Cotton Mather had published a book about witchcraft in 1689. Samuel Parris owned it. Some in Salem Village, including the children, could have been persuaded by its contents.

ergot fungus

Cotton Mather wrote a second book about witchcraft and the Salem witch trials in 1693 called *The Wonders of the Invisible World*. It defended the trials.

Cotton Mather

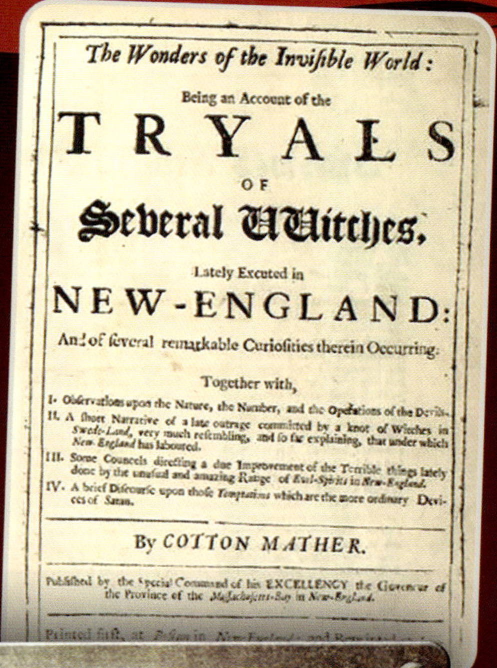

The Wonders of the Invisible World:

Being an Account of the

TRYALS

OF

Several Witches,

Lately Excuted in

NEW-ENGLAND:

And of several remarkable Curiosities therein Occurring.

Together with,

I. Observations upon the Nature, the Number, and the Operations of the Devils.

II. A short Narrative of a late outrage committed by a knot of Witches in *Swede-Land*, very much resembling, and so far explaining, that under which *New-England* has laboured.

III. Some Councels directing a due Improvement of the Terrible things lately done by the unusual and amazing Range of *Evil-Spirits* in *New-England*.

IV. A brief Discourse upon those *Temptations* which are the more ordinary Devices of Satan.

By *COTTON MATHER*.

Published by the Special Command of his EXCELLENCY the Governour of the Province of the *Massachusetts-Bay* in *New-England*.

COTTON MATHER

Cotton Mather was a respected Puritan minister in colonial New England during the time of the trials. He wrote a letter to one of the magistrates that warned him to be careful of using spectral evidence to convict someone. He also offered other unreliable ways to detect witchcraft.

AFTERMATH

By the time the Salem witch trials were over, more than 170 people had been accused. Nineteen had been hanged, one had been crushed to death, and at least five more died in the poor conditions of the colonial prisons, including the baby of Sarah Good. It didn't take long for the wider world to realize the injustice of the trials.

By 1702, the General Court of Massachusetts admitted that the proceedings went against the law for many reasons. In 1711, Massachusetts exonerated, or declared not guilty, many of the convicted and gave their families money. In 1992, the Salem Witch Trials Memorial was completed in Danvers, Massachusetts.

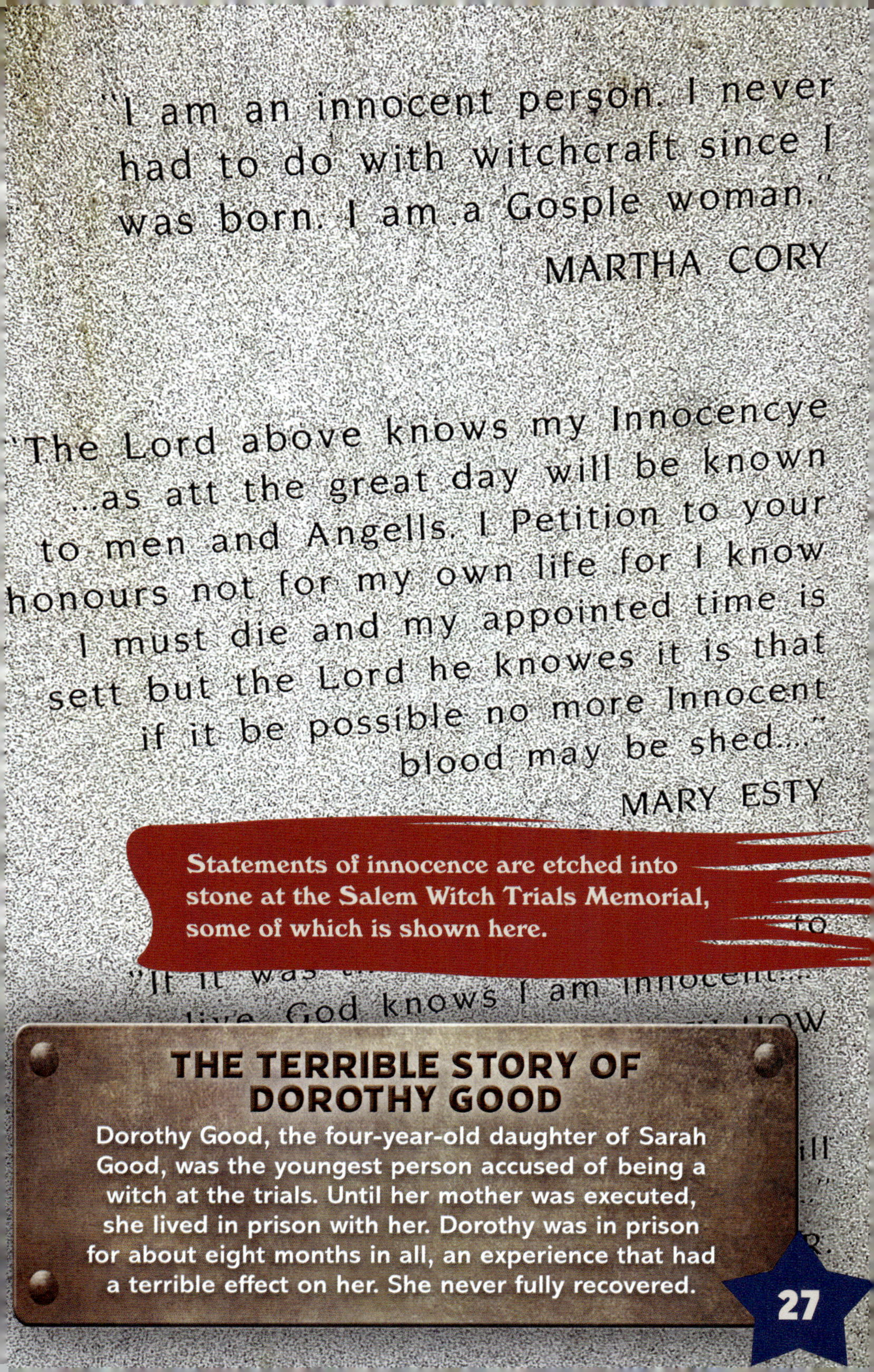

Statements of innocence are etched into stone at the Salem Witch Trials Memorial, some of which is shown here.

THE TERRIBLE STORY OF DOROTHY GOOD

Dorothy Good, the four-year-old daughter of Sarah Good, was the youngest person accused of being a witch at the trials. Until her mother was executed, she lived in prison with her. Dorothy was in prison for about eight months in all, an experience that had a terrible effect on her. She never fully recovered.

THE LAST WITCH

In 2022, more than 300 years after the trials, the last of the convicted, Elizabeth Johnson Jr., was exonerated of witchcraft. This was thanks to the studies of an eighth-grade class in Massachusetts, who realized she was the only person who hadn't been declared innocent over the years. They petitioned, or formally asked, the Massachusetts state government to exonerate Johnson, who had said she was told to confess to save her life.

This tragic chapter in colonial history still draws people to Massachusetts. The terrible toll of the dead and the destruction of lives, families, and a community should forever be remembered.

The house of magistrate Jonathan Corwin still stands in Salem. It's called "Witch House" today.

TIMELINE OF THE WITCH TRIALS

1692

January: Betty Parris and Abigail Williams show odd behaviors.

February: The girls accuse three women—Sarah Good, Sarah Osborn, and Tituba—of being witches.

March: Tituba confesses and names the other two women as witches. She says other unknown community members are witches too.

May: Osborn dies in jail.

June: Bridget Bishop is the first person hanged for witchcraft.

July: Five people, including Rebecca Nurse and Sarah Good, are hanged.

August: Five more people are hanged.

September: Giles Corey is pressed to death after refusing to enter a plea. Eight more people are hanged.

October: The Massachusetts governor ends the special court.

December: A new Superior Court is set up. Spectral evidence isn't allowed.

1693

January: The court convicts three people of witchcraft.

May: All convicted of witchcraft have been pardoned.

CHANGES IN THE LAW

The Salem witch trials would have ended differently today. First, the accused were presumed, or believed, to be guilty. Today, accused people are presumed to be innocent. In addition, the Salem judges allowed hearsay evidence, or statements about facts made out of court. This isn't allowed today. Finally, accused people today have the right to be represented by lawyers, who weren't allowed in the Salem witch trials.

GLOSSARY

chaotic: In a state of total confusion with no order.

convicted: Found guilty in a court of law.

fungus: A living thing that is somewhat like a plant, but doesn't make its own food, have leaves, or have a green color. Fungi include molds and mushrooms.

hallucinate: To seem to see, hear, feel, or smell something that doesn't exist.

magistrate: A person who acts as a judge in a court of law, usually for less serious crimes.

marginalized: Having to with someone or something being treated as if they aren't important.

medieval: Having to do with the Middle Ages, a time in European history from about 500 to 1500.

pamphlet: A small book that gives information.

prominent: Well known or important in some way.

spectral: Seeming to be or be from the spirit of someone.

supernatural: Unable to be explained or seeming to come from magic.

testimony: Evidence that a witness gives in court.

FOR MORE INFORMATION

BOOKS

Cooke, Tim. *Accused of Witchcraft! Salem, 1692-1693*. Minneapolis, MN: Bearport Publishing Company, 2023.

Fitzpatrick, Insha. *Who Was Accused in the Salem Witch Trials? Tituba*. New York, NY: Penguin Workshop, 2023.

Peterson, Megan Cooley. *The Salem Witch Trials: Spot the Myths*. North Mankato, MN: Capstone Press, 2024.

WEBSITES

Kid Questions
salemwitchmuseum.com/kids-questions/
The official Salem Witch Museum answers questions from kids.

The Salem Witch Trials
kids.nationalgeographic.com/history/article/salem-witch-trials
See illustrations and review the events of the Salem witch trials.

Salem Witch Trials
www.ducksters.com/history/colonial_america/salem_witch_trials.php
This site breaks down the facts as well as how the "evidence" presented at the trials.

Publisher's note to educators and parents: Our editors have carefully reviewed this website to ensure it is suitable for students. Many websites change frequently, however, and we cannot guarantee that a site's future contents will continue to meet our high standards of quality and educational value. Be advised that students should be closely supervised whenever they access the internet.

INDEX

Bishop, Bridget, 18, 29
Burroughs, George, 19
Corey, Giles, 20, 21, 29
Corey, Martha, 20
Corwin, Jonathan, 13, 29
Court of Oyer and Terminer, 15
Danvers, Massachusetts, 5, 19, 26
exonerations, 26, 28
Good, Sarah, 12, 13, 18, 26, 27, 29
governor, 14, 22, 29
Griggs, William, 11
Johnson, Elizabeth, 28
magistrates, 12, 13, 25, 29
Mather, Cotton, 24, 25
Nurse, Rebecca, 14, 18, 19, 29
Osborn, Sarah, 12, 13, 29
pardon, 22, 29
Parris, Betty, 10, 11, 29
Parris, Samuel, 8, 9, 10, 11, 12, 14, 24
peine forte et dure, 20
Puritans, 9, 25
Putnams, 8, 14, 18
Salem Witch Trials Memorial, 26, 27
spectral evidence, 16, 17, 22, 23, 25, 29
Tituba, 8, 9, 12, 13, 14, 29
Williams, Abigail, 10, 11, 29
Witch House, 29
witch hunts, 4, 6, 7
women, 5, 7, 13, 14